How to Protect Our Children

In School

Warning Sign Checklists

Quick Reference Guide

(Step by Step Revised Edition.)

For Busy Parents, Law Enforcement, School Staff and other Professionals…

It Could Save Their Lives…

By Daphne Lichter

Published by
Lichterbooks

Copyright 2009
By Daphne Lichter

Library of Congress Cataloging in Publication Data

Author: Lichter, Daphne
How to Protect our children in School (It Could Save their Lives...) A Step by Step Guide for busy parents and professionals (Revised Edition)

ISBN 978-0-96745601-0

Contents

IF YOU NEED IMMEDIATE ASSISTANCE, DIAL 911.

**For information about
crime prevention programs,
Call your local police department.**

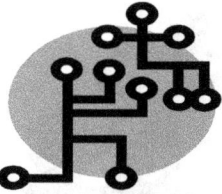

AUTHOR'S NOTE

The idea for the **Quick Reference Guide** of "HOW TO PROTECT OUR CHILDREN IN SCHOOL (IT COULD SAVE THEIR LIVES)" - came to me when parents and professionals requested a shorter version of the original book. While helping kids and families link up with resources, I discovered that no matter where kids went to school, parents were often in the dark as to their "secret lives."   They were often not aware of the warning signs in "at risk kids" that are predictors of school violence. This **Quick Reference** guide could help identify the warning signs of "red flags in children" such as abuse, alienation, depression… A concerned parent and or professional could then help predict and prevent violent incidents, before they occur. Today, it has become clear that, with the rampages happening too often on school grounds, something must be done. Kids today have easy access to everything including: guns, drugs, violent movies, video games, music, and unsupervised internet use. Most communication between kids today is done through electronic devices and on networking sites on the internet. (myspace.com , face book.com, you tube…) They post information and pictures in their profiles that would make many an adult uncomfortable. This is the norm and the reality for so many kids today. The good news is that these days, the details of a child/teen's personal life is easily accessible for anyone who takes the time to look. Kids have gone hi-tech. They post information about themselves intended for their "friends" but easily available to "anyone". They seem to believe that if they delete information from their phones, internet sites, it is gone. Unfortunately, for them, but luckily for parents, law enforcement and professionals, the information is still there and can be retrieved, if needed. It is amazing to me that kids today believe their communications with each other are invisible to the rest of us. Drug deals, gang activities and school fights are just a few of these "invisible to adults" activities that occur in schools on a daily basis. School fights are often scheduled in advance, on the web. Students chat with their "friends" and "dare" their perceived "enemies" Then, the fight is scheduled, often on school grounds and everyone involved shows up to fight or to watch.   These "at risk" kids, which professionals are trying to identify, put the rest of the students in danger on school grounds. It is difficult for hardworking students to study and succeed when there is an underlying feeling that they are not safe in school. This Quick Reference guide is an attempt to help parents and professionals uncover the secret lives of kids today, detect problems through the warning signs checklists, and seek help, as needed. Supervising their internet use and paying close attention to the communications on all their electronic devices will make you more aware of the "reality" of their daily lives. They probably have a personal profile and pictures on their social networking sites. You might ask them to see it to make sure you are comfortable with what they are posting online and on their electronic devises. You may know about "texting" but not be aware of "sexting activities" (exchange of inappropriate pictures of themselves with chat logs to their "friends") You may be surprised to find out that knowing more about the details of their daily lives may be a relief to them. They may not have felt safe at school and had no way of letting you know about it without breaking the code of silence with their "friends" The need to be loved and to belong to a peer group is very powerful. It may lead kids to make bad decisions out of fear that there is no one who can help them, if needed. The information is available, for anyone to see. If you pay the bills, you should be able to see the details of your account and activity of anyone using it.(including your children).

We are the adults and we can help lead kids to a productive, successful life!

INTRODUCTION

Calling all parents and professionals! The slayings at Columbine High School in Littleton, Colorado have riddled at the core of our collective consciousness nationally and internationally. The attacks in schools involving kids killing kids have sparked debates from The White House to every house on the causes, warning signs, and ways to stop or at least predict the violence in schools. There is a consensus that this could happen again, anywhere, anytime. Everyone must take personal responsibility to help kids succeed in school in a safe environment; free of fear, bullying and violence. Getting hurt or even killed on school grounds are just some of the concerns facing kids today. Regardless of the causes that lead kids to hurt and or kill other kids, there are some facts we can no longer ignore. Over 6,000 students were expelled last year nationwide for taking guns to schools. Those expelled were the ones who were caught. What about the students who brought guns to school and just fell through the cracks of the system? Such daily exposure to fears of survival, whether real or magnified, make it harder for students to concentrate on what it takes to succeed in school. Whether your child is in public, private, charter or home school, you want to make sure he/she is not only learning skills necessary to graduate but is also adequately prepared for college and "life". The second edition of "How to Protect Our Children in School" is a Quick Reference guide to identify some of the Warning Signs that are predictors of violence in children/teens. You can then seek help, as needed. Kids today communicate with each other through their electronic devices and the internet. They have gone hi-tech! Everything they say, do and plan is probably stored on one of their electronic devices and or posted somewhere on the internet. Chances are, most of the details of their personal lives are posted with pictures of themselves on networks such as my space.com, face book.com, you tube.com and others, for all to see. A parent and or a professional can easily find out information about the secret lives of kids by knowing where to look!

If you are aware and vigilant, you can help them, if needed!

PART 1

STEP BY STEP QUICK REFERENCE GUIDE

(At least 5 things you can do…)

STEP 1:

KEY FACTS: *Understand the System*

WHY? Understand how The Public School System works can help you reach your goal of making it work for you.

HOW? There are six facts you must know that can help you to get the System to work for you.

1. The Public School System is a bureaucracy where everyone is accountable to someone. Schools are accountable to school boards which are subject to state statutes. School boards are accountable to school districts which are either elected or appointed. School districts answer to the state cabinets which often double as departments of Education. The states answer to the federal U.S. Department of Education which provides 7% of funding to the states. **This can work in your favor by allowing to climb the "ladder of accountability" until you can climb up the chain of command until you find the right person who is willing and able assist you.**

2. The Public School System offers free compulsory education for about 12 years, depending on the state you live in.
This fact helps you realize that you are entitled to an education suited for your child.

3. The Public School System offers many different schools and programs. Included, are elementary, middle, and high school, which are part of a much larger system. Vocational, adult, gifted, gifted, learning disabled, emotionally handicapped, and magnet programs are just a few examples of the vast amount of choices available. **The key is to find out what is available and how to get your child in the right program.**

4. **There are no national standards for education.** Principals from different schools have different standards and rules. Education not only varies from state to state but from school to school. **If your child is not doing well in one school or program, it is usually possible to get him/her transferred to a different program and/or a different school to achieve better results.**

5. There are 16,000 school districts, 65 million students, 2.5 million teachers, and 1 counselor for every 800 kids in the United States today. By sending your child to a different school/program, you may drastically change the standards and regulations your child must adhere to. If you change school districts, the change may be even more drastic.

6. If you have a concern about the quality of education that your child is receiving, you are not alone. Many others across the country have similar concerns about unsafe schools, low academic standards and other issues. **There is someone in the system who is the right person to address your particular concern and has the authority to do something about it. The right person can help!**

KEY FACTS:

Understand the system (cont...)
Key facts to remember:

➢ Start at your school with your principal to address your concerns.
  Before starting to climb the ladder of accountability, request a copy
  of all your child's records so you can refer to them as you contact the
  different organizations.
➢ To make your school accountable, go to the school board. Make sure
  you have the names of all the people you talked to and the dates and
  times that the conversations took place.
➢ To make the boards accountable, go to the districts with all the
  names of the people you talked to and the dates of the conversations.
➢ To make the district accountable, go to the state with all the names of
  the people you talked to and the dates of the conversations.
➢ To make the state accountable, go the U.S. Department of Education.
➢ Get everything in writing.

STEP 1:
Understand the System
TAKE CONTROL!

Sample Letter: Request for records from your child's school

Date_____

To Whom it May Concern:

My child, _____is having problems keeping
his/her grades up. I am considering hiring a tutor to assist him/her
improve study habits. Under the Federal Privacy Act, I am requesting
copies of all school records to be made available as soon as possible,
so I can forward them to the tutor.

I am also requesting that my child be put on a daily or weekly
progress report to monitor progress. Please inform the teachers
of the efforts to be made by the student and parents. If there are any requests
from the teachers to give extra homework for my child to help him/her improve
performance, please include them in the progress report.

Thank you for your cooperation. I can be reached at the following
numbers/email_____

Sincerely,

Parent

Cc: Principal
     School Board-Superintendent (get name)

STEP 2:
Solve That Case!

WHY USE THE LADDER OF ACCOUNTABILITY?
⇨ By understanding how the system works, you can make it work in the best interest of your child.

⇨ You will know how to find out which programs and schools are available in your area.

⇨ It will allow you to determine which schools and programs fit your child and how to avoid the pitfalls of the system.

⇨ BECAUSE:
⇨ In a bureaucracy, everyone has a job to do.

⇨ Usually employees are only familiar with their own jobs, not with the whole system.

⇨ For every rule, there is an exception and someone authorized to grant it.

⇨ Find the person who knows the answer and can hold your school accountable.

⇨ The higher up you go in the ladder of each system (local, state, federal) the more administrators care about image and how the whole system works.

⇨ Top level administrators are elected or appointed and want to stay in office.

⇨ Never fight. Your goal is to find out who can and is also willing to help!

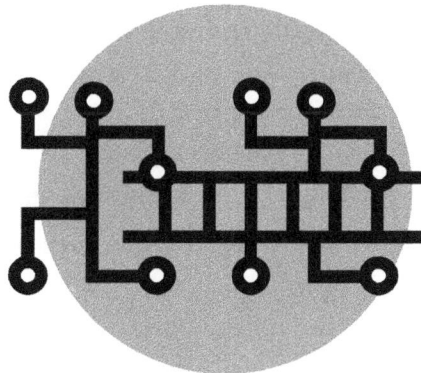

STEP 2: Solve That Case!

Ladder of Accountability
(The Public School System)

START HERE:

⇨ Step 1	Step 2	Step 3	Step 4	Step 5
Your school	*School Board*	*Local District*	*State*	*Federal*

Rules for using the Ladder of Accountability

Rule 1: In a bureaucracy, everyone is accountable to someone.

Rule 2: Your school is accountable to the School Board
School Board is accountable to the School District
District is accountable to the State
State is accountable to Federal

Rule 3: If you do not get satisfaction, you start at the school (step 1)
and climb the "Ladder" until you get your answer.

STEP 3:
Set the Standard:
Choose a School and Program!

When it comes to the education of a child, parents need to know they have choices. To get a high school diploma, there are many routes you can take to reach your goal. The Public School System is the most obvious (paid with tax dollars); but there are other options. Private schools, charter schools, and home-schooling are just some of the other avenues to a diploma.

If you miss out on any of these opportunities, you can also take a G.E.D. which is an emergency test that that will also lead to a diploma allowing you to get into most colleges.

STEP 3:Set the Standard (cont…)

THE RIGHT SCHOOL/PROGRAM
CASE STUDY

Boy, age 14, was bright, outgoing, and in his mother's words, "a model child". He was bored in class, had stopped doing his work, and was rapidly falling behind. The mother said her son was only interested in one thing since he was 2 years old, marine life and fishing. Since there was a magnet school for marine biology in the area, I suggested that he apply. Before applying, the mother called the principal of the magnet school and advised her of her son's failing grades. She also told her that her son enjoyed everything to do with marine life and hoped there would be a spot for him in the school. The mother asked what her son's chances were of being accepted. The principal replied" "Don't even bother to apply. His chances with failing grades is nil." Discouraged, the mother asked me what to do in place of this marine biology program. I told her I felt he belonged in that school and in the marine program. I told her I would check the "state" criteria for entrance. He did meet the criteria (grades had little to do with eligibility) , was accepted to the program and is as happy as a fish in water.

Lessons to be Learned:

NEVER ACCEPT THE WORD OF ANYONE, UNTIL YOU SEE IT IN PRINT!
Entrance criteria all different and one item such as grades, as in this case, carries a small number of points in the overall list of criteria.
Some people do not mind giving you incorrect information, for a variety of reasons; it is against their own interests. (In this case, the principal may have felt that she had enough applicants and did not want to be bothered with additional ones.)
I have observed in my work as a tutor, that obstacles along the way can be overcome by knowing who to call for help.
There is someone out there who is willing and able to help!

STEP 4:
Make a Choice:
Test for Learning Disabilities
 by Dr. Sarah Allison

Definition:
"Learning disabilities is a general term that refers to a heterogeneous group of disorders manifested by significant difficulties in the acquisition and use of listening, speaking, reading, writing, reasoning, or mathematical abilities. These disorders are intrinsic to the individual and presumed to be due to central nervous system dysfunction. Problems in self-regulatory behaviors, social perception and social interaction may exist with learning disabilities, but do not by themselves constitute a learning disability. Even though a learning disability may occur concomitantly with other handicapping conditions. (e.g. sensory impairment, mental retardation, social and emotional disturbance) or environmental influences, (e.g. cultural differences, psychogenic factors) it is not the result of those conditions or influences"

National Joint Committee on Learning Disabilities, 1994, pp.65-66

"You cannot put the same shoe on every foot."
Syrus Maxim
596

WARNING SIGNS CHECKLIST
Learning Disabilities
- Problem concentrating
- Impulsive
- Inattentive
- Distractible
- Shorter attention span than non-disabled peer
- Difficulties in processing information and communicating
- Memory - long term/short term
- Poor planning and organizing skills
- Difficulty in studying, utilizing time efficiently, and organizing
- Behavior problems
- Hyperactivity
- Social skills problems
- Reading problems
- Written language problems
- Math problems
- Social and behavioral problems

Recommendations:
- *Must be trained to focus attention to process information.*
- *Must use memory strategies.*
- *Create solutions by formulating new answers related to intelligence level.*

If you suspect a learning disability, get your child tested. A child with a learning disability will be teased and further alienated by peers.

Take the first step—get help!

(Get a check-up: Physical - Hearing - Eyes.)

Schedule a check-up: Physical, Hearing , Eyes
REQUEST FOR TESTING

Sample letter

Date_____

To Whom it May Concern:

My child, _____, is experiencing problems paying attention in class. I took him/her
for a physical examination and he/she checked out fine. His/her eyes and hearing
were checked and everything was normal.

To determine his/her problem, I am requesting testing from the school district.
Please test for gifted and all learning disabilities.

Please inform me immediately of the procedures for testing.

Thank you for your assistance.

Sincerely,

Parent
1 copy: to school
1 copy: to school board.

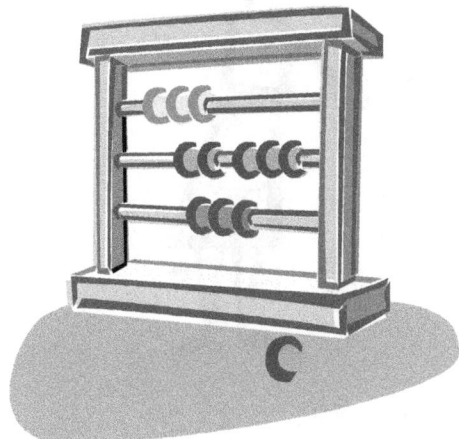

STUDY SKILLS:

"MINDS ARE LIKE PARACHUTES. THEY ONLY FUNCTION WHEN THEY ARE OPEN"

SIR JAMES DEWAR
1842-1923

STEP 5:
STUDY SKILLS

There is no magic formula to good study habits. However, if a student is motivated to do well and achieve certain goals, success can be achieved. There are several skills that should be mastered to gain good study habits. The bottom line is learning to study smarter, not harder.

The basic skills necessary for good study habits are reading, comprehension, memory, retention, classroom participation, test preparation, note-taking, writing papers, library skills, time management, and consistent work habits.

After you determine which of the skills your child has and which he/she needs to improve, you look for assistance to acquire the necessary skills. There are many options available besides hiring a private tutor. You could ask for a referral from your teacher/school for "free tutoring". (subsidized government program)

Remember:

SHOWING UP IS 80% OF SUCCESS!

• STUDY SKILLS CHECKLIST

- Time management skills (planning homework assignments and tests.
- Organizational skills (use of a calendar)
- Memory: remembering what you read
- Comprehension: understanding what you read
- Test Preparation
- Consistent study habits (studying at a set time whether you feel like it or not)
- Note-taking
- Showing up for class
- Class participation
- Doing your homework

- <u>MATERIALS NEEDED AT HOME:</u>
- Calendar
- Watch
- Place to study
- Good lighting

- <u>WHAT KIDS NEED AT SCHOOL:</u> (POSITIVE ATTITUDE)
- Books
- Paper, pen, pencil
- Watch
- Class participation
- Sit in front of class
- Come on time
- Ask questions
- Be prepared for tests
- Bring homework to class

Part 2

Identify problems by using
Warning sign checklists
Quick Reference Guide

- ➢ Identify problem
- ➢ Tell someone who can help child and family.(school, Police…)
- ➢ Follow-up to see if child got appropriate help

Warning Signs Checklist:
Quick Reference Guide
For Parents/Educators/Law Enforcement

Abuse(Physical, Emotional, Sexual)

Witnessing or experiencing abuse is a very important predictor of future criminal behavior.

- **Domestic Violence calls to the home**
- **Anger and/or rage**
- **Depression**
- **Self-mutilation**
- **Self-destruction and /or destructive behavior**
- **Low self-esteem**
- **Anxiety**
- **Excessive fear**
- **Secrecy**
- **Sexual behavior not age appropriate**
- **Abusing someone else**
- **Being a bully, especially towards girls or smaller, weaker children**
- **Problems concentrating in school**
- **Failing Grades**
- **Physical signs of bruises and or cuts**
- **Telling someone of the abuse**
- **Feels unsafe (looks for protection in a gang or with older kids)**
- **Running away**
- **Torture of family pets or other neighborhood animals or creatures such as frogs, birds, etc…**

If you suspect abuse, report it. It is the law. Tell someone who can help the child/family. (school, police,) The situation will be investigated by the proper authorities. You could follow-up to see if child got appropriate help.
YOU COULD BE SAVING A LIFE!

Warning signs checklist:

Quick Reference Guide
For Parents/Educators/Law Enforcement

Alienation in Teens:

- Anger or rage
- Excessive Internet us (using any electronic device to connect to others: looking for web sites and/or groups with similar feelings of rage and hatred)
- Joining a gang
- Excessive vulnerability to peer pressure
- Obsession with violence (music, movies, video games…)
- Fascination with guns and explosives
- Talk of suicide and /or homicide
- No respect or trust of authority or rules
- Hopelessness
- Secrecy and mistrust of Adults
- Looking to be noticed in a negative or positive way
- Friends with similar ideas and behavior
- No sense of purpose
- Double life(1 life with parents and 1 secret life with other kids)
- Feel parents do not really want to know what they are doing or thinking (too busy with their own lives)
- Not involved or concerned about helping others
- Not accountable for their own behavior (do not feel there are consequences for their actions)
- Low self-esteem (do not belong to the in- crowd; feel rejected and persecuted
- Cruelty to animals

Alienation is the feeling that one is alone. Many children feel very alone. Whether they turn to substance abuse to mask their pain and/or gangs to meet the need to have an identity and belong, they are trying to stop the feelings of alienation. Broken families and lack of extended families seem to shatter a child's world and reinforce the feeling that adults are not to be trusted. They seem to live for today, with no thoughts for their future, or consequences to their actions. Internet web sites with organized hate messages seem to attract loners who look to connect and justify their feelings of rage and alienation. Add video and violent media exposure to the equation and we have violence just waiting to erupt. Kids have gone hi-tech. They do use their electronic devices and social networking sites to communicate with each other. **Take time to check their profiles, chat logs and internet posts and find out more about your child's secret life.**   22

Warning signs checklist:

Quick Reference Guide

For Parents/Educators/Law Enforcement

Communication breakdown in Child/teen
Parents:

- You consistently use the following roadblocks to good communication: Ordering, Probing, Judging, Sarcasm, Commanding, Threatening, Preaching, and Moralizing
- You fail to understand the meaning of what is being said
- You are not interested in the thoughts of your child
- You are not interested in the feelings of your child
- You fail to put your child high on priority list of your life
- You do not mirror back what your child/teen is trying to say
- Child/teen shows warning signs to alert you to a problem (see checklists)

Child/teen:

- Fails to establish eye contact
- Does not listen
- Interrupts and disrupts
- Wants to hurt you and others
- Spends excessive time on the internet and using electronic devices to communicate with peers.

Communication is the sharing of thoughts and feelings. The closer the communication, the stronger the bond between the parties. When communication breaks down, everyone feels alienated, angry and alone. Good communication is the key to finding out what is truly going on in your child's/teen's life. Listen to your children and watch out for the warning signs that will help you detect problems before they occur. It is easier for parents to communicate if they learn to use the electronic devices your children are using. If you take the initiative, you can learn to nag electronically! When you contact them via text, request they respond within a reasonable amount of time if they want to keep their phone! If you pay the bill, you should be able to set the rules and conditions about using it.

Warning signs checklists:

Quick Reference Guide

For Parents, Educators and Law Enforcement

Depression

- **Feeling of sadness lasting more than a few weeks**
- **Isolation; staying in his/her room all day**
- **Crying spells**
- **Acting out**
- **Alienation from family and friends**
- **Breakdown of communication with family and friends**
- **Thoughts or expressing thoughts of self-mutilation, ending one's life, or speaking of homicide**
- **Lack of interest in activities once enjoyed**
- **Change in sleep patterns (too much sleep, too little sleep.)**
- **Magnifying of personal problems**
- **Feelings of persecution ("everyone is out to get me")**
- **Lack of energy**
- **Running away-truancy**
- **Failing grades**
- **Hopelessness for personal future**
- **Giving away personal possessions**

Depression in teens can be very serious. Suicide is the second leading cause of death among teens. In most cases, guns were used, so remove weapons from the house if your child/teen is depressed. Depression is treatable in 80% of the cases, so get help!

Warning signs checklists:
Quick Reference Guide
For Parents/Educators/Law Enforcement

Gangs

Your child may be involved with a Gang:
Uncover his/her secret life

- Dressing in on style all the time
- Tattoos, jewelry (colored beads), emblems, wearing certain colors
- Change in school performance
- Grades drop
- Staying "out" for no good reason
- Association with know gang members or recruiters (I.e., young girl and older boy)
- Carrying weapons or caught with weapons at school
- Use of special hand signals
- Use of special codes while sending text messages on cell phone
- Use of cellular phones in school
- Graffiti on notebooks or walls
- Found with unexplained large sums of money
- Excessive internet use
- Excessive electronic devices use
- Severe body bruises or unexplained injuries from a beating might indicate gang initiation
- Loyalty to friends above all else (friends before family)
- Excessive truancy(look for skipping after roll call)
- Secrecy-especially on phones and other electronic devices
- Multiple sex partners
- Criminal behavior (shoplifting, theft gang members collect assets)
- Excessive fear (may feel they cannot leave the gang)
- Frequent fights at school (fights are often scheduled in advance on the internet)
- Alienation of friends and family

Today's gangs are armed, more aggressive, and traffic in drugs. Gangs are not just an inner city problem any longer. The F.B.I. believes there are over 400,000 gang members in 700 cities throughout the United States. Gangs operate in 94% of the cities. Once your child is bonded to a gang, it may be very difficult to convince them to leave. **If you suspect your child is involved in a gang, contact your local Police Department for help. Most have a gang task force who are trained to help you help your child and family. The Gang Resistance Education Training (G.R.E.A.T.) program is a federal program developed to assist law enforcement agencies in their efforts to fight gang violence.** 25

Warning Signs Checklists

Quick Reference Guide

For Parents/Educators/Law Enforcement

Involving Possible Substance Abuse

- Sudden poor or failing grades
- Loss of interest in extracurricular activities once enjoyed
- Sudden weight loss, no appetite, or eating excessively at various non-traditional times
- Smoking of cigarettes or cheap cigars
- Drug paraphernalia lying around (pipes, lighters, rolling papers, eye drops, small plastic bags, tin foil rolled or crunched up, prescription drugs missing)
- Truancy (cuts classes and inconsistent attendance)
- Change in appearance and change in hygiene (fails to bathe regularly, brush teeth and hair); wears clothes and underwear for several days. Sloppy, worn look for look for certain music groups known to advocate drug usage.
- Signs of depression
- Excessive influence by peers
- Lack of respect for authority
- Secrecy
- Excessive internet use (could be on social networks; myspace.com posting images, pictures, messages related to drug use and dealing)
- Change in sleep habits (cannot sleep during normal sleep hours)
- Missing money, credit cards and or valuables (items that can be easily pawned or sold)
- Irresponsible behavior (disappears for hours without calling or stays out all night)
- No conscience (addiction needs come before choosing right from wrong)
- Lack of attention, slow responses to questions or requests to do certain things. *Be aware of-*Marijuana; Pot, Grass, Weed, Reefer...**Cocaine;** Coke , Snow, freebase, crack rock...**Heroine;** junk, horse ,**Hallucinogens**; PCP, LSD, Ecstasy , designer drugs...**Sedatives;** downers, prescription pain pills...**Amphetamines**; Methamphetamine , speed, uppers...

Warning Signs Checklists
Quick Reference Guide
For Parents/Educators/Law Enforcement
Suicidal Tendencies in Child/Teen

- **Depression**
- **Isolation**
- **Thoughts of Suicide**
- **A suicide plan told to someone (a cry for help)**
- **Hopelessness for personal future**
- **Giving away personal possessions**
- **Fear of not meeting expectations of parents or other significant others**
- **Magnifying problems**
- **All or nothing thinking**
- **Feelings of persecution**
- **Feeling one is not loved or needed ("Everyone is better off without me")**

Suicide is the second leading cause of death in teens aged 11-17. Over 5,000 teens die each year from suicide. Depression is one of the first signs and is treatable 80% of the time. Remove guns from the house if you suspect you have a depressed or suicidal child/teen. Get help if you suspect your child/teen is suicidal.

Warning Signs Checklist
Quick Reference Guide
For Parents/Educators/Law Enforcement

Truancy;

Greatest predictor in adolescence of future criminal behavior…

- **Poor or failing grades**
- **Drug use**
- **Gang affiliation**
- **Unexcused absences**
- **Repeated suspensions**
- **Running away**
- **Criminal behavior**
- **Lack of respect for authority and or rules**
- **Friends with similar behaviors**
- **Parents who do not know where their kids are (kids hide kids)**
- **No value on education**
- **Hopelessness for personal future**
- **No interest in extra-curricular activities and or sports once enjoyed**
- **Excessive internet use (includes excessive time spent on electronic devices)**
- **No perspective (live for today)**

Punishment does not stop truancy. Suspensions make the problems worse because the kids fall behind and give up. Look for alternative suspension programs through the schools and police departments in your community.

Warning Sign Checklist

Quick Reference Guide

For Parents/Educators/Law Enforcement

UNSAFE SCHOOLS

- Graffiti not removed promptly
- No metal detectors
- Electronic devices allowed on school grounds
- No random checks of lockers , bathrooms and classrooms for drugs and weapons
- Drug-free, Gun-free, Bully-free zones are not enforced
- No Dress code
- Students are allowed to leave during lunch
- No I.D. badges for visitors, staff, teachers and students to identify them as part of the school.
- School police do not cooperate or report to local police department incidents of truancy, drug use, weapon found. Incidents are handled internally.
- At risk students are not identified and referred for help. (no screening of depressed or angry students.)
- Fights and gangs are allowed to operate on school grounds, triggering behavior that leads to escalated violence.
- No zero-tolerance policies on gangs, drugs, weapons, bullying and violence on school grounds.
- No accountability or consequences for students who have committed offences (suspension is just a slap on the wrist)
- No new background checks on teachers/staff/ who have been transferred from a different school and have a record.

You can help improve the safety of your school by forming partnerships between parents, schools and law enforcement. You can make a difference by working together! A school is as good as it's principal. He /she has the authority to make the necessary changes to make the school safer. Try to designate a key contact person to coordinate your efforts.

Appendix 1
Gun Safety

Some facts you should know…

- According to the experts, kids can get firearms just about whenever and wherever they want
- Kids get most of their guns by breaking into homes and cars
- Over 7000 guns are stolen each year from the glove compartment of cars
- 42% of boys between the ages of 17-19 admit to carrying firearms or being with someone who does, or playing with guns when their parents were not home
- Most teenage suicides occur with guns.

Appendix 2
The Internet (and other Electronic Devices…)

Kids today have gone hi-tech. They communicate with each other on the internet via social networking sites (I.e. myspace.com , face book.com. you tube.com, twitter…) and via their electronic devices. (cell phones…) They usually post their profiles, pictures, personal information on a giant bulletin board called the internet for all to see. Often, if you ask them they are oblivious to the fact that they are not "invisible". Once their information is posted and pictures forwarded, there is a record that can be retrieved, if needed. That is great news for parents, guardians and law enforcement not for the ones who flaunt their private lives for all to see! It might be wise for those who do not read the terms of use of some of these sites and agree to them to think before signing on the dotted line electronically. The internet is not regulated and is still like the "Wild West". Anything goes and the user has usually agreed to let their information be sold to the highest bidder!

Sexual predators browse the chat room on social networks looking for victims. That is one of the greatest dangers for kids today. Teach your kids not post any personal information on the internet that could get into the wrong hands. (photos, birthdays, phone numbers, addresses, names…)

By keeping up to date on the ways kids communicate with each other, you can help keep them safe on the internet and their electronic devices.

Acknowledgements

- Thanks to Diana L. the bravest and sweetest person I know. You are beautiful inside and out. Always stay so loyal and true. You are my precious sweetie. I love you.
- Thanks to Deborah L. You set the standard for the rest of us for overcoming adversity and coming out a "winner". You are my pride and joy. May all your dreams come true. If someone is intelligent enough to sort it all out and do it, it is you! I love you.
- Thanks to Dahlia L. You set the standard for hard work, determination and self discipline. Your precious "babies" and loved ones are so lucky to have you as an inspiration in their lives. I love you.
- Thanks to my Mom who has always protected me. I love you.
- Thanks to Morris Peer, my wonderful father for showing me how to diffuse a difficult situation with humor. You were always on my side. I love you and miss you so much…
- Thanks to Edna and Ori, for giving me hope to explore new possibilities for a happy life. I love you.
- Thanks to Sunny and Nikita for showing me the meaning of unconditional love. I love you and miss you.
- Thanks to Sharon S., for your friendship and loyalty. I turn to you for words of wisdom. You are my rock and precious friend.
- Thanks to Dr. Einat B. Cohen, my childhood friend who has always inspired me by personal example, to lead a meaningful life.
- Thanks to Dr. Regina Shearn, my mentor and friend. You give me hope…
- Thanks to Dr. S. Allison, my friend ,who has always been there for me.
- Thanks to Gila M. my friend who gives me hope on a daily basis.
- Thanks to Rose Chapman, my friend who has always been there for me.
- Thanks to Ryan Chapman. You are to me "the kid who grew up right" You set the standard for the rest of us for compassion and sensitivity.
- Thanks to Dale Michelson, my friend who has always been there for me.
- Thanks to Ray Irons for always having my back and being on my side.

www.ingramcontent.com/pod-product-compliance
Lightning Source LLC
Chambersburg PA
CBHW081258110426
42743CB00045B/3338